# IF YOU TRAVELED
# On the
# Underground
# Railroad

With special thanks to Dr. Reine Cartel Jackson, Associate Professor at Wellesley College.

Text copyright © 2022 by Ebony Joy Wilkins
Illustrations copyright © 2022 by Steffi Walthall

Library of Congress Cataloging-in-Publication Data Available

ISBN 978-1-338-78891-4 (paperback) / ISBN 978-1-338-78892-1 (hardcover)

10 9 8 7 6 5 4 3 2 1      22 23 24 25 26

Printed in China    38
First edition, November 2022

Book design by
Jaime Lucero and Brian LaRossa

# If You Traveled
# On the
# Underground
# Railroad

Written By
**Ebony Joy Wilkins**

Illustrated By
**Steffi Walthall**

**SCHOLASTIC PRESS** • **NEW YORK**

# Table of Contents

# Introduction

If you traveled along the Underground Railroad, you would have **embarked** on one of the most secret and dangerous trips of your life. The Underground Railroad operated during a **tumultuous** time in United States history, after millions of innocent African people were chained together and stolen from their homelands, **enslaved** in the Americas, and forced to work in life-threatening conditions.

Attempting to run away to **freedom** was dangerous and nearly impossible. It was illegal for enslaved people to learn

to read, write, marry, carry guns, gather in large groups, or even **protest** against their enslavers. However, many of the African people consistently fought back to regain their freedom and used the Underground Railroad **network** to escape the torture of **captivity**. What was the Underground Railroad? Who traveled on it? Was it a real railroad? This book will reveal answers to those questions and more.

# What was slavery?

**Slavery** was the practice of forcing humans into unpaid labor for the monetary benefit of others. In 1501, white enslavers arrived by boat on the west coast of the African continent to force thousands of innocent African people,

including men, women, and children, onto large ships bound for Santo Domingo. This journey became known as the **Middle Passage**. Those captured were the first of hundreds of thousands of people who would be forced out of their homelands to work in foreign lands. The African people were chained together with tight metal clamps on their necks, hands, and feet; **branded** with hot irons on their skin; beaten with whips and batons; and then crammed into the **bilge** of the ships for a journey that could take weeks or months and would forever change their lives.

The bilge area of the ship was tight, stuffy, uncomfortable, and unsanitary. The enslaved people were denied room to stretch their muscles or even clean their bodies. Most had never traveled on open waters before. The boats rocked continuously and sometimes violently. Some would not survive the monthlong trip across the Atlantic Ocean. Others would arrive in the Americas sleep-deprived, starved, and sickly. Enslaved people were brought to many different lands. They were separated from their parents, children, siblings, and community members. They could not communicate with their enslavers or other enslaved Africans. Language barriers caused great confusion. The journey had been **brutal**, and the treatment by their captors was even worse.

Despite the enslaved people's now-frail condition, their enslavers remained focused on the potential for **financial** gain. The captured and now-enslaved Africans had been tricked, dragged from their homes, and stripped of their names, families, and all **human rights** so that their enslavers could use them as unpaid laborers to maintain their wealthy lifestyles.

Once they arrived at their destination, the enslaved Africans were then placed on auction blocks in front of men and women who paid money for them. Each enslaved person was considered the property of the enslaver, and they were then expected to work from sunrise to sundown for free for the rest of their lives. Any children they bore were also enslaved and expected to work on the **plantations**. This included tending to beans, rice, or cotton crops in large fields; cooking and cleaning in the enslaver's home; maintaining the property; and caring for the family who owned them. If they refused to work or fought back in any way, they were beaten, starved, or sold away to other families. Enslaved people were expected to follow all directions from their enslavers.

Though the working and living conditions were extremely harsh and often unbearable for enslaved people, the practice of slavery continued for hundreds of years. In 1619, captured African people were first brought to Jamestown, Virginia. They were disoriented. Nauseated. Scared. They could not communicate with their captors. They were confused. They were hungry. They were tired. They did not know this would not be the worst part of their journey. It was only the beginning of nearly 250 years of slavery in what would become the United States.

# What was the Underground Railroad?

From the first moment families were stolen away from their communities in Africa, there were men and women who tried to escape from their captors. Some fought back before they were shackled together with chains. Some jumped overboard while crossing the Atlantic Ocean. Those who made it to the Americas to be sold to the highest bidders often ran away at the first chance they got. The escapes were not without serious risk. These men and women were under constant surveillance, with the threat of torture or even death if they disobeyed their enslavers. Running away could cost them their lives. Escaping required planning and a network of freedom supporters who could provide safety while they ran.

In 1831, an enslaved man named Tice Davids was being held and forced to work on a plantation in Kentucky. One day, he saw an opportunity to leave. When the plantation owners and the **overseers** learned of Davids's escape, they tried to recapture him and return him to bondage. Davids

swam across the Ohio River with men following behind him in boats. But somewhere along his escape, Davids found people who took him into hiding. The men following him lost track of him and returned to the plantation angry. Davids had made it to freedom in Ohio. His enslaver decided he must have gone underground somehow.

A few years later, in 1839, something similar happened again. An enslaved man named Jim ran away from a plantation where he was being held, and the men following him lost sight of him, too. It was like he also had disappeared. After several more escapes like Tice's and Jim's, with enslaved people going underground, word got out about a network of antislavery supporters who had joined together to help them hide from their captors. They created a secret network of safe locations so that enslaved people could move undiscovered across the country to freedom. In the 1840s, this network to freedom became what we now call the Underground Railroad.

# Was the Underground Railroad a real railroad?

There were routes. There was travel. There were passengers. But the Underground Railroad was not a physical railroad or train. The Underground Railroad was actually a network of people who helped freedom seekers escape from slavery. The network of Good Samaritans consisted of people who wanted to and were able to help enslaved people. They created routes of safe houses to hide freedom seekers. Before the Underground Railroad, each enslaved person was running by themselves, often in the dark of night. When word began to spread that there were people against slavery who were willing to help the freedom fight, they no longer had to escape all on their own.

Each location along the Underground Railroad, called a station, provided safe harbor for enslaved people who were escaping to freedom. Freedom seekers hid in the basements of churches, in the back rooms of schoolhouses, in hidden rooms inside private homes, and outdoors in the woods,

caves, and even marshes. With the help of **conductors** and railroad workers, those running could move on foot, in hidden compartments of horse-drawn carriages, on newly invented steam engine trains, or in small boats. They moved from one underground station to the next until they made it to places where slavery was outlawed. Once they reached freedom, the African people formed new communities called maroon communities. But in order to start over in these new maroon societies, they first had to risk their lives using the Underground Railroad.

# Why is it called the Underground Railroad?

The stations operated just like a real train station. There were routes, station workers, and conductors, but only certain people knew about them. It was too dangerous to try to run away from the plantation in broad daylight. There were overseers watching. There were other enslaved people working

nearby. The plantation owners were also on the property. It was safer to travel during the night, under the cover of darkness and out of sight of anyone who would report their disappearance. Fleeing from the plantations in the dark of night was still dangerous, though, without the help of the Underground Railroad.

The enslaved people who escaped moved throughout the night on a specific schedule created so that their captors would not be able to catch up to them. When morning rose and the plantation owners and overseers learned that someone had escaped, they sent a search party after them. Dogs tracked the freedom seeker's scent. Overseers had whips to punish the freedom seekers if they were found. The workers on the Underground Railroad communicated with one another and pointed the freedom seekers in the direction of each next safe location, just like a conductor would do on a real train. Each safe house was connected to the next. Most of the freedom seekers were leaving from the South and heading north, where slavery was less prevalent and even outlawed in some places.

It didn't take long for news to spread, by word of mouth and through songs, about the mysterious underground travel that could lead to freedom. As the network grew, more enslaved people were able to escape to freedom.

# Why was the Underground Railroad important?

Slavery was big business. European and American enslavers were not motivated to help free anyone. They were only concerned with making money by selling people or by selling the goods that enslaved people planted and gathered to other enslavers. They were not concerned with the safety of their workers or the families of the workers. Enslavers were allowed to treat their workers as they saw fit, so there was no motivation to allow their freedom. It was even illegal for enslaved people to try to escape. Because slavery was a legal business at this time, the Underground Railroad was one of the only options that enslaved people could use to free themselves.

Some freedom seekers did leave without the help of the Underground Railroad. Before the Underground Railroad became well known, enslaved people risked freedom by hiding on boat docks and sneaking onto ships heading north. They borrowed the required identification papers from fellow enslaved people, or even squeezed their bodies into large containers and mailed themselves all the way to freedom, like one enslaved man in Richmond, Virginia, named Henry Brown. But without the safe houses along the Underground Railroad, enslaved people would be putting themselves in greater danger. The Underground Railroad offered a safer and more organized way for enslaved people to fight against an unjust system.

Because the conditions were life-threatening, freedom was always on the minds of enslaved people. The Underground Railroad gave freedom seekers the opportunity to find and reconnect with their family members, culture, and identity. It also gave them the chance to rebuild their lives as free men and women.

# When and how did the Underground Railroad start?

The first ships carrying captured Africans landed in North America in 1619. Those captured were filed off the ships and onto auction blocks to be sold to the highest bidder. Their teeth, hair, skin, and body parts were examined in front of large crowds. Plantation owners waited to bid so that they would have workers to maintain their property.

From the beginning, there were enslaved people who fought back and prayed for an opportunity to escape to freedom. The Underground Railroad was born out of those prayers. As soon as the first enslaved person successfully made it all the way to freedom in Northern states, a network began to form. As word spread, both free and formerly enslaved people joined the movement. There were also members of faith organizations who wanted to see an end to slavery in all states. Together, they created a network to help those who were ready to regain their freedom.

Though the Underground Railroad started as soon as African people were first sold into slavery, it was not named officially until the 1800s. One early example of this developing freedom network was formed in 1839. A woman named Harriet Powell arrived in Syracuse, New York, with the family who enslaved her in Mississippi, the Davenports, when she was fourteen years old. Many people in Syracuse assumed that Harriet was a family member, until several free Black residents of the town began asking her questions. When they learned that Harriet was not a member of the family or there of her own free will, they grew concerned. They put together a plan to free her.

While the Davenports were distracted with friends, Harriet was able to slip away. The Syracuse residents, including a man named Thomas Leonard, shuttled her between safe houses. They sent her first to Syracuse House

and then to the homes of John Clarke and Gerrit Smith so that she would not be found. The Davenports were not happy at all about Harriet's disappearance. They formed a search party and offered a two-hundred-dollar reward for her immediate capture, but the residents of Syracuse were steps ahead of them. They

worked together to move Harriet around the city until she could safely make it to freedom in Canada. Harriet would still have to be careful up North. If caught, she risked being sent back into enslavement.

When word got back to the Davenports that Harriet was in Canada, they pushed for stronger fugitive slave laws that would later be **enacted**. The network of supporters in Syracuse was just getting started. Harriet was one of many enslaved people who would reach freedom with the aid of the network.

# Who traveled on the Underground Railroad?

Men, women, and children who were escaping their enslavers traveled along the Underground Railroad. They had already been repeatedly separated from family members in Africa and in America. They continued to face that threat daily on the plantations where they were forced to work. At any time, and for any reason, they could be sold away to a new plantation and never see their families again. The threat was overwhelming and devastating.

When they made the decision to try to escape their enslavers, they trusted guides like Harriet Tubman, William Still, and David Ruggles to lead them to freedom. While Tubman alone rescued more than seventy people, there were many others who helped guide enslaved people to freedom. There were also many other freedom seekers who left and attempted to reach a safe house without the help of a conductor. Not everyone made it to freedom.

HARRIET TUBMAN

WILLIAM STILL

DAVID RUGGLES

# Who operated the Underground Railroad?

Conductors, also called guides, helped to lead freedom seekers from safe house to safe house. Some guides along the Underground Railroad were formerly enslaved. They knew firsthand the risks of running away and the fear of being hunted down by teams of men with guns and dogs. A man named Jermain Loguen knew the danger of running away. He had escaped from a plantation in Tennessee and used the Underground Railroad to reach freedom in Canada. He didn't stay in Canada for long. He returned to the South to rescue his family so that they could start a new life in Syracuse together. He also had a heart for helping others and served

JERMAIN LOGUEN

as an African Methodist Episcopal minister. He used his ministry to spread the word of God and used the church as a station on the Underground Railroad.

There were many other conductors on the Underground Railroad. The network was supported by men and women of all races, including **abolitionists**, ministers, freed people, farmers, and business owners who supported freedom efforts. It was rare to see people of different races working together during this time. **Segregation**, or separation, by race was more the norm, and was often required by law. When it came to rescuing enslaved people, though, everyone was welcomed and needed. Conductors came from all walks of life and used all the resources that they had to help free people.

# Who was William Still?

William Still helped so many people escape from enslavement that he became known as "the father of the Underground Railroad." He provided aid to more than eight hundred people, inviting them into his home, documenting their stories, and raising money to support rescue missions for other conductors, like Harriet Tubman.

WILLIAM STILL

As a young boy, Still understood the pain of family separation and the importance of helping others. His mother, Charity, had to leave two sons behind when she ran from a plantation in Maryland with two of her daughters. His father, Levin, was eventually able to buy his freedom and find his way back to them.

The Still family resettled on a farm in Burlington County, New Jersey, where William was born. When he was a young boy, he rescued his first enslaved man and committed the rest of his life to abolitionist work. His efforts saved many, including his brother Peter. William taught himself to read and write, and became a successful author, businessman, and clerk.

In his writings, Still included stories and photos of his family, and recounted rescues of enslaved people from Philadelphia to Ontario. He also spoke frequently on the rights of formerly enslaved people. He supported organizations like the Pennsylvania Society for the Abolition of Slavery and the Pennsylvania Civil, Social, and Statistical Association, organizations committed to helping formerly enslaved people resettle, vote, and work.

# Who was David Ruggles?

David Ruggles was born in Norwich, Connecticut, in 1810. His parents, David Sr. and Nancy, taught him and his six siblings to work hard and fight for others. Following their lead, David attended a religious school and dedicated his life to helping others.

Ruggles was an abolitionist, writer, publisher, and **mariner**. He used his resources and talents to open a grocery, which also

became the first Black-owned bookstore and reading room, where he welcomed African Americans who were fleeing, researching, organizing, and resettling. His writings included *The Mirror of Liberty* and other antislavery works.

Ruggles helped six hundred people escape to freedom, and supported abolitionists like Frederick Douglass, Sojourner Truth, and William Cooper Nell. His antislavery work drew attention from those who needed his help running away, but it also attracted the attention of white men who tried to silence him on more than one occasion.

He believed in confronting enslavers who tried to kidnap freed men and illegally sell them into slavery. His confrontations included civil disobedience and self-defense. This was dangerous work, even for a free man, and his life was often in danger. He was physically assaulted and almost kidnapped. A mob of white enslavers burned down his store in 1835, but Ruggles remained determined to fight back. He acted as secretary of the New York Committee of Vigilance, which helped formerly enslaved men and women to build new lives after slavery.

## Who was Harriet Tubman?

Harriet Tubman, born Araminta Ross, was the most well-known conductor on the Underground Railroad. Before she escaped to freedom, she lived with her family on the Brodess Plantation in Maryland. In 1844, she married a free Black man named John Tubman and changed her name to Harriet Tubman. She dreamed of running away from her life of enslavement.

Tubman often put her own life on the line to save others, even in the face of danger. When one enslaved person on the Brodess Plantation tried to flee and was caught, Tubman stepped in the way of their punishment. She took the blow of a large weight that was thrown at them. The weight struck her in the head. She was badly hurt, but she was never taken to the hospital for treatment, and the wound was never attended to. Her only choice was to live with the pain and seizures that followed. She was sent back into the fields to work, but she did not let her pain distract her from her desire to escape.

One day, in 1849, Tubman learned that she may be sold to another plantation owner. This meant she would be taken away from the people she knew and loved forever. She had already watched three of her sisters be sold away to new plantations, and she did not want the same thing to happen to her. Tubman devised a plan to run away before that could happen.

Tubman was able to convince two of her nine siblings to escape with her. When work on the plantation ended for the day and the fields were clear, Tubman and her brothers made a run for it. They used the stars and moonlight to guide them deep into the woods and away from trouble. This first trip was too much for her brothers, though. There was too much unknown outside the plantation. The chances of getting caught and punished were too high, and they convinced their determined sister to turn back.

But Tubman was not done running. She refused to be sold away. She wanted to leave on her own terms, so she set out again a few days later. This trip was a success. She made her way through Maryland to Delaware and Pennsylvania before settling in Philadelphia. Against the odds, she had made it safely to freedom by herself. She could have made a good life for herself as a freed woman in Philadelphia, but she had left too much behind. She wanted to save her family back in Maryland. So she went back to get them.

Tubman also wanted her husband, John, to join her in Philadelphia. She returned to the Maryland plantation safely two years after her original escape, but by the time she returned, he had already remarried another woman. John chose to stay with his new wife and would not leave with Harriet. Even though her husband refused to leave, that did not stop Tubman from helping the rest of her family and many others to freedom.

Tubman continued to risk her new life as a freed woman to save others. She made so many successful trips on the Underground Railroad that runaway enslaved people began referring to her as "Moses" in reference to a character in the Old Testament.

# What did Harriet Tubman do?

Today, Harriet Tubman is primarily remembered as a conductor on the Underground Railroad. She guided seventy enslaved people safely from Maryland to freedom in Canada. "I was the conductor of the Underground Railroad for eight years, and I can say what most conductors can't say—I never ran my train off the track and I never lost a passenger."

Word started to spread about Tubman's skills. She was small in stature, but she had an excellent memory, calming voice, and fearless nature. She also knew the South well and could be trusted with private information, which got the attention of Union army officials. They asked Tubman to serve as a soldier and spy during the Civil War when it began in 1861. Tubman used her expertise at moving around unnoticed to lead several important covert missions to uncover information and rescue people.

One of her most successful missions was the Combahee Ferry Raid. On June 1, 1863, Tubman teamed up with Colonel

James Montgomery to save more than three hundred enslaved people in South Carolina. President Abraham Lincoln had issued the **Emancipation Proclamation** six months earlier, freeing all enslaved people in the South. But many enslavers kept this information from those they enslaved so they would not lose money. Once the people at Combahee heard the news, they made plans to leave as soon as they were able to.

Tubman and Montgomery hoped to free those who remained in enslavement and recruit many of them to the Union army. Early in the morning of June 2, Tubman, Montgomery, and three hundred Union soldiers began their mission to rescue the freed men and women. Their arrival on the plantation brought gunfire, confusion, and total chaos. In the midst of uproar, Tubman was calm. She began

46

to sing, her voice reassuring those around her and guiding the people toward her and to the waiting Union army boats. In the end, seven hundred people were freed through her actions. Many of them went on to join the Union army.

Although Tubman's efforts serving the Union army were well known, she was never rightfully **compensated** for her work because she was Black and because she was a woman. Even as a freed person, she had to fight to be recognized and paid fairly for the work that she had done. For many years she appealed to the government to pay her for her services. While she waited for payment and recognition, she started her life over again. She spent her time after the Civil War opening a washhouse and working as a laundress. Later in life, she joined the **suffrage movement**. She died in 1913.

# Who was Frederick Douglass?

Frederick Douglass was a formerly enslaved man who became a writer, editor, speaker, and abolitionist. Though it was illegal, he had taught himself how to read and write while enslaved as a child. As an adult, he used his talent to tell others about what he experienced while he was enslaved, as well as about his time as a conductor along the Underground Railroad. His first book, an **autobiography** called *Narrative of the Life of Frederick Douglass, an American Slave, Written by Himself*, was published in 1845.

In 1847, Douglass moved his family to Rochester, New York. It was there he started *The North Star*, a newspaper devoted to antislavery work. In addition, his home became a station on the Underground

FREDERICK DOUGLASS

Railroad, where he welcomed freedom seekers while they were trying to start newly freed lives.

Douglass began sharing his writing and experiences as widely as he could, but that was dangerous. Because he had escaped, appearing in public increased his chances of being recaptured and returned to enslavement. He toured different cities, and even countries like England and Ireland, to tell his story. He wrote so well that he and his supporters were able to negotiate his freedom by paying the man who had enslaved him.

Douglass did not stop at sharing his story. He also fought to have Black soldiers allowed into the Union army and became a recruiter during the Civil War. By the time slavery came to an end, he had helped nearly four hundred freedom seekers escape to Canada by way of the Rochester ferry. After the Civil War, he continued to work toward the goal of equality for the newly freed men and women. He died in 1895.

## Where did the Underground Railroad operate?

The Underground Railroad operated in every direction of the US, from north to south and from east to west. But not all states were safe for enslaved people to run to, including those declared as free states. In 1820, the Missouri Compromise determined which states would continue to support slavery and which states would outlaw slavery. Missouri remained in support of slavery, while Maine became a free state. Free states included the Northern states of Ohio, Indiana, Illinois, Michigan, Iowa, Wisconsin, and Minnesota. States farther south like Alabama, Arkansas, Delaware, Florida, Georgia, Kentucky, Louisiana, and Mississippi continued to support slavery.

But even if a state outlawed slavery, it didn't mean it was always welcoming to freedom seekers. Most enslaved people who were kept on plantations in Southern states wanted to run toward Northern states, or to Canada, where slavery had

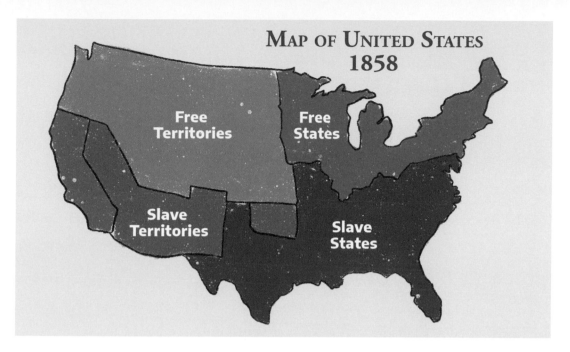

MAP OF UNITED STATES
1858

Free Territories

Free States

Slave Territories

Slave States

been outlawed in 1834. There were other options for freedom seekers who were enslaved in the Deep South. They could run farther south to Mexico, the Caribbean Islands, and to other spots outside the US.

There were guides and safe houses ready along each coast, and there were routes for enslaved people heading in every direction. The goal was to reach secluded maroon communities of freed Black people, where everyone was welcomed and focused on starting new lives away from enslavement.

## How did the Underground Railroad operate?

Running away to a new life required a lot of planning, courage, assistance, and supplies. It was imperative for freedom seekers to remain hidden until they had safely reached freedom. Keeping them fully hidden was difficult and costly, though. Underground Railroad supporters formed abolitionist societies that were able to provide assistance and supplies for freedom seekers by offering lectures about antislavery efforts. During these lectures the abolitionists would collect donations and money to help continue their efforts. Donations also came from schoolchildren and various goodwill and hobby groups.

Enslavers were determined to track down, recapture, and punish freedom seekers who tried running away. There was often a **bounty**, or a price given in exchange for capture, set for those who were on the run.

Most freedom seekers left the plantations during the

dark of night, often having to trudge through wooded areas, cross bodies of water, travel secret paths, and hide in tunnels until they reached an awaiting conductor. The guides used a secret sign language, spread by word of mouth and through songs, to alert freedom seekers that it was safe to reveal themselves. Temporary safety spots included churches and houses with hidden doorways, underground tunnels, and secret passageways. When freedom seekers reached the safe houses, they were given medical attention, food, clothing, transportation, routes, and enough supplies to continue on to the next station on the Underground Railroad.

## Where were the Underground Railroad stations located?

There were many hidden stations along the Underground Railroad. Each station provided temporary **respite** for freedom seekers. There was no consistent length of time that freedom seekers stayed at each location. Some stayed only one night, while others had to stay for days at a time until it was safe for them to move on to the next safe house. The stations stretched in many directions and were also located along water transportation routes so that some could escape

on small boats. Others could remain safe inside homes, churches, or carriages, out of sight of those chasing after them.

Those running north were guided through the New York State cities of Ithaca, Cayuga Lake, Auburn, and on to Oswego. One route used water transportation up the Hudson River Valley through Albany, Syracuse, Watertown, and then to Canada. Freedom seekers who ran from Ohio and Pennsylvania were guided along routes that went to Indiana, Iowa, and on to Buffalo and Rochester, New York. In the northern port cities of Oswego and Rochester, guides snuck freedom seekers onto boats heading to Canada, where they were welcomed by allies with supplies and freedom.

## How did the Underground Railroad travelers find the stations?

There were no written maps for enslaved people to consult as they were traveling to each station. When the decision was made to run, they first had to learn what and who to look for once they stepped foot outside the plantation. Sometimes they would be under the watch of a conductor, but other times they would have to move from station to station on their own. So they used word of mouth and songs to teach one another the code needed to safely travel. By the time they were ready to go, they knew how to proceed. Passing news about the railroad could be dangerous. Those who knew how to read and write had to do so secretly, sharing news through songs and stories that often contained secret messages. Some of those messages included news about formerly enslaved men and women running away from the plantations and making it north to free lands. Anyone wanting to escape using the Underground Railroad had to wait for word from conductors and faith leaders that the roads were clear and safe enough to travel.

While running, freedom seekers had to be on the lookout for search parties of dogs and men who wanted to recapture them, but also look for clues and secret messages left by conductors at each location. There were some more visible markers, like flashing lights, marked trees, lit lanterns, painted chimney bricks, and waving flags. Some sounds also served as indicators of safety, like the repeated tapping of small stones, quiet knocks on doors or windows, and secret passwords spoken from one person to the next. Each sign meant that there was a safe place to hide, travel, gather, or find food.

## Did a trip along the Underground Railroad cost money?

Conductors at each station did not expect payment in exchange for providing safety to freedom seekers. They **volunteered** their homes, boats, and food because they believed slavery was wrong and they wanted to help freedom seekers in any way that they could. Even though freedom seekers did not have to pay money, the price of freedom was still high.

Freedom seekers were risking their lives. They were unprotected, vulnerable, and scared. Leaving the plantation also meant leaving their family and friends—again. They said goodbye to enslavement, but also to people who would have to remain behind. Some would return to try to rescue others, but many never would.

Unfortunately, not all freedom seekers made it. Some were captured by bounty hunters, beaten, and returned to captivity. Others fell prey to freezing temperatures or unexpected illnesses. Some were even killed for daring to run in the first place.

# Why was escaping on the Underground Railroad difficult?

Escaping from slavery was difficult for enslaved people for many reasons. Legally, they were bound to their enslavers. Running away meant breaking the law and risking their lives.

There were overseers who were hired to keep watch over the workers on the plantations. If the work was not done or was done too slowly, they were punished. Those who ran had to do so secretly. Their absence could not be noticed until they were hidden a safe distance away. Once they were discovered missing, the overseer, plantation owner, hunting dogs, and other nearby landowners were notified and set out to find and recapture them. If they were found, they were punished, and sometimes permanently wounded.

The best time to escape was at night, but this was also dangerous. The terrain was often unfamiliar and unforgiving. Enslaved people had few resources or supplies and often had to flee at a moment's notice. They layered what torn clothing they had and walked into the night with no shoes, no coat, and little food. They had to move on foot as quietly as possible. Even the snap of twigs could alert bounty hunters to their location. There were wild animals roaming at night. Strangers could stop and question Black people at any time and for any reason. They were required to have signed permission

documenting that they were allowed to travel. If they did not provide this paperwork, they could be captured and returned to the plantation they were fleeing. Once they arrived back on the plantation, they were punished, often in public to scare others who might be thinking of running away.

For enslaved people, no help was coming to them. Running was the only option. But they would not be able to make the long journey to freedom alone. They would have to rely on strangers, often non-Black strangers, to help guide them from safe house to safe house. Trusting non-Black people while they were on the run was terrifying. If they followed one wrong person, they could be recaptured and returned back to be tortured. They had to hide their tears. But freedom seekers had to take the risk. Traveling slowly, one day at a time, was not easy. Freedom seekers were heading from state to state and had to watch their every move until they reached a free state. This amount of travel could take weeks or even months, but the reward of making it to freedom was worth every risk.

# Who was against the Underground Railroad?

There were many who supported the freedom seekers making it to free and safer lives through the Underground Railroad. But politicians, enslavers, and those who had invested money into the business of slavery wanted to stop the Underground Railroad as soon as it started. The Underground Railroad was bad for their businesses. The more people they could keep enslaved, the more money there was to be made. And that money came with power.

Freedom seekers who did make it to free states began to push back against the business of slavery and fight for their freedom through the justice system. Hundreds of people sued for their freedom. One couple named

DRED AND HARRIET SCOTT

Dred and Harriet Scott filed lawsuits asking to be considered free in the eyes of the law. Dred Scott was owned by a man named John Emerson who lived in Missouri, a state that allowed slavery. Emerson moved around while in the military and took Scott with him while residing in the free states of Illinois and Wisconsin. When Emerson married, he moved his family and the people he enslaved back to Missouri. Scott attempted to purchase his freedom from the Emerson family but was denied. He did not give up his fight for freedom. Instead, in 1846, he sued for his freedom. Together with his wife, Harriet, the couple decided to sue for her freedom as well. The cases were combined and *Scott v. Emerson*, and later *Scott v. Sanford*, would be considered by the courts.

The battle for freedom continued for years. The Scotts argued that they should be considered free because they had resided with the Emerson family in Illinois and Wisconsin, both free states. The judge disagreed and declared they could not be considered free because they later returned to Missouri, a proslavery state. The judge believed African Americans

should never become citizens of the United States and therefore should have no ability to vote, sue, or have rights of any kind. However, the **jury** ruled in 1850 that Scott had won his freedom. It didn't take long for that verdict to be overturned. Scott sued again, this time through the federal courts. Seven years later, the US Supreme Court decided that African Americans could be citizens of certain states, but they could not sue the federal court and could not be citizens of the United States.

According to people who supported slavery, enslaved people were not considered human beings and did not deserve freedom. Therefore, enslaved people had no legal rights.

## What was the Fugitive Slave Act?

Enslavers were so upset about enslaved people running away and about losing money from their labor that they pushed for additional laws to punish anyone who tried to run or anyone who attempted to help freedom seekers. They wanted new laws that would compensate them more and further punish freedom seekers. To that end, lawmakers passed the first Fugitive Slave Act in 1793. This law made it much more difficult for enslaved people who were trying to escape to freedom and for anyone trying to help free them. Enslavers and bounty hunters were offered money to recapture any freedom seekers that they could find, not just the ones they enslaved, and even if they were found in free states.

Now this meant even more danger to those running for their lives. Any citizen could capture them at any time. They could be discovered at any time. They could be killed at any time. The act also required the government to step in to help harshly punish runaway enslaved people and those who helped them escape. The pressure to remain hidden was intensified again.

## Was anyone hurt while traveling on the Underground Railroad?

Life as an enslaved person meant living under the constant threat of harm. On the plantation, an overseer or plantation owner could whip, beat, or **maim** anyone they deemed deserving. On the run, a plantation owner could recapture a freedom seeker, or a hunting dog could catch up and bite them. The Underground Railroad provided a way out, but it was not a ticket out of harm's way. Traveling along the Underground Railroad was dangerous and often life-threatening. One wrong step and someone could be hurt. Plantation owners sent men with guns after the runaway enslaved people. When the runaways, gun-toting men, and hunting dogs collided, many people got hurt. Many enslaved people were whipped. Many were beaten. Those who tried to run off were treated even worse than they had been before. Some were even killed.

# When did slavery end?

Many people continued to make money off the backs of enslaved people, even after 1808, when the United States instituted a ban on the trading of enslaved people from Africa. Thirty years later, slavery was ended in England, Jamaica, Barbados, and other West Indian Territories, but continued in the United States. It would be twenty-five more years before President Abraham Lincoln took a stand. The Dred Scott Decision in 1857 supported the continuation of abuse against African people. According to the US Supreme Court, African Americans could never be citizens and Congress had no authority to end slavery. So enslavers continued to buy, sell, and abuse African people. Enslaved people continued to fight back and run when they could.

On January 1, 1863, during the Civil War, President Lincoln signed the Emancipation Proclamation to encourage now-freed Black people to join the Union army in the Civil War. Though the Emancipation Proclamation ended legalized slavery in the Southern states, slavery continued full steam ahead in states that remained within the Union. Two years later, slavery was abolished fully in the United States when the 13th Amendment to the Constitution was **ratified**. But this decision did not come easily, and not everyone recognized the amendment.

# When did the Underground Railroad stop running?

Slavery was abolished in 1865. While the 13th Amendment ended legal slavery, illegal slavery would continue for many years because of greed, **racism**, and money. Some enslaved people would not hear of their freedom until many years after they were legally freed because their enslavers continued to make money and wanted to maintain power. Those committed to the freedom of all people would keep going until everyone was freed.

Even though some were still enslaved, the Underground Railroad was no longer needed. Freeing enslaved Africans did not have to happen in secret or underground anymore. And on June 19, 1865, a general in the Union army announced that slavery had ended as he rode through Galveston, Texas, two years after the Emancipation Proclamation had freed all enslaved people in the South. This day became known as Juneteenth, a word combining the month and day, which commemorates freedom for enslaved people in the United States. Juneteenth is a federal holiday that is celebrated annually throughout the United States.

## Conclusion

Thousands of Africans were stolen from their homelands and sold into captivity in the Americas. Many would suffer their entire lives while working in treacherous conditions under the watchful eye of their enslavers. Those who attempted to free themselves and reconnect with their families could be caught, severely punished, and sometimes even killed. Some were able to connect to the Underground Railroad network

of caregivers who guided them to freedom. Word started to spread quickly about the Underground Railroad by word of mouth and through songs. More enslaved people were running away, which angered enslavers who were losing money. They had to pay high prices to capture any enslaved person who attempted to run. Their goal was clear: to continue the practice of slavery.

The Underground Railroad was a lifeline. This network of people operated until slavery was legally abolished in 1865, when the 13th Amendment declared that enslaved people were free. Once freed, African families were free to resettle and start over on their own terms. However necessary, the fight for freedom and the ability to resettle did not come easily, and continues even today. The United States was built on the backs of African people who have not been repaid or compensated for their suffering or work.

The Underground Railroad may be part of history now, but the fight for freedoms and **reparations** for African people and their descendants lives on.

## Additional Reading

**Cline-Ransome, Lesa, and James Ransome.** *Before She Was Harriet*. New York: Holiday House, 2019.

**Dunbar, Erica Armstrong.** *Never Caught*. New York: 37 Ink, 2017.

**Dunbar, Erica Armstrong.** *She Came to Slay: The Life and Times of Harriet Tubman*. New York: 37 Ink, 2019.

**Hopkinson, Deborah, and James Ransome.** *Sweet Clara and the Freedom Quilt*. New York: Dragonfly Books, 1995.

**Levine, Ellen, and Kadir Nelson.** *Henry's Freedom Box*. New York: Scholastic, 2007.

**Nelson, Vaunda Micheaux, and Colin Bootman.** *Almost to Freedom*. New York: Carolrhoda Books, 2006.

**Ringgold, Faith.** *Aunt Harriet's Underground Railroad in the Sky*. New York: Crown, 1992.

# Glossary

**Abolitionists:** those who were in favor of ending slavery and freeing enslaved people

**Autobiography:** a written account of a person's life in their own words

**Bilge:** basement level of a ship

**Bounty:** an amount of money given to someone as a reward for catching a criminal

**Branded:** marked or burned with a symbol onto skin

**Brutal:** extremely cruel or harsh

**Captivity:** the state of being kept in a place and not being able to leave

**Compensated:** gave someone money to repay something they lost

**Conductors:** people who operated safe houses and stations along the Underground Railroad

**Emancipation Proclamation:** an announcement made by President Lincoln freeing all slaves in states fighting against the Union; went into effect on January 1, 1863

**Embarked:** began a journey, especially on a ship or airplane

**Enacted:** made into an act or statute

**Enslaved:** to be held in slavery or bondage

**Financial:** relating to money

**Freedom:** the state of being free; the right to be or go somewhere without being controlled

**Human Rights:** the rights that every person should have regardless of their sex, race, or religion

**Jury:** a group of people selected according to the law to render a verdict, or true answer, concerning a cause or accusation submitted to them

**Maim:** to injure or hurt causing permanent damage

**Mariner:** a sailor, someone who makes a living on the sea

**Middle Passage:** the journey that forced Africans onto ships that sailed across the Atlantic Ocean

**Network:** a group of people or organizations that are closely connected and that work together

**Overseers:** people who supervise workers

**Plantations:** large farms or estates for the cultivation of cotton, tobacco, coffee, sugarcane, etc., typically maintained by enslaved, unpaid, or low-wage laborers

**Protest:** an expression or declaration of objection, disapproval, or dissent, often in opposition to something a person is powerless to prevent or avoid

**Racism:** racial or ethnic prejudice or intolerance

**Ratified:** confirmed by expressing approval

**Reparations:** monetary or other compensation payable by a country to an individual for a historic wrong

**Respite:** a delay or cessation for a time, especially of anything distressing or trying; an interval of relief

**Segregation:** the act or practice of segregating; a setting apart or separation of people or things from others or from the main body or group

**Slavery:** the practice of owning enslaved people

**Suffrage Movement:** the seventy-two-year-long battle for women's right to vote in the United States, 1848–1920.

**Tumultuous:** involving a lot of violence, confusion, or disorder

**Volunteered:** performed a service willingly and without pay